FROM pain TO Praise

FROM pain TO Praise

An Inspirational Collection

KATHY M. WALTERS

Golden-Browne Publishing Company
Atlanta, Georgia

Cover Design: Damon Danielson/Divine Image Graphics
Author's photo by: Derrick Wills/ID Graphics, Inc

Golden-Browne Publishing Company
P.O. Box 162114
Atlanta, Ga. 30321
Printed in the United States of America
First Paperback Edition
ISBN 978-0-980227-2-2-2
LCCN 2013933389

Contents

Part 1: Don't Ever Stop Dreaming, Praying and Trying

Part 2: Bradford

Part 3: In Her Own Words . . .

Part 4: My Pen, My Paper, My Heart . . . My Story

Part 5: Cathartic Creations: The poetic cleanse

Part 6: Pillars of Positivity

Part 7: Positive Perspectives

Part 8: Pills for Your Pain

Part 9: Pensive Pause

Part 10: Path to Progression

For Everyone

From Pain to Praise

I can't give up

Though impossible to comprehend

The depth of how even my soul has tears

Thirsting for the peace and the joy left behind

This plight has weakened me

Consuming my mind

So I continue to pray

More and more each day

No matter the negatives I face

I press; I prevail in spite of the delay

God's favor leads from pain to praise!

-Kathy M. Walters

~ Thoughts from the Author ~

*O*ften times in life, we go through changes, phases and stages. Some are good, some are bad. Some appear to set us back while others make us grow or even set us free. The most important thing to remember is that everyone is either going through, in the midst of, or coming out of a storm, no matter how well put together we may appear to the world. It is easy to see others and feel as though they have it all together. It is easy to drive through a brand-new subdivision and become so engrossed with the aesthetics of a home and the front-yard view. Unbeknownst to you and me, the back yard and inside of the home are a total disaster! Sometimes what we perceive from looking in from the outside is a remarkably deceptive portrayal of reality. Until we are given the opportunity to see how things really are, we have no earthly idea what people are going through or the types of battles or challenges they, too, are trying to overcome.

Remember the movie *Soul Food*? Shortly after the opening of the movie, we saw what appeared to be a normal, everyday family. The Sunday dinner table was set with macaroni and cheese, collard greens, cornbread, black-eyed peas and all the fixings. Teri, Bird and Maxine all joined in to help "Mama Jo", more affectionately known as "Big Mama", prepare the traditional soul food dinner.

Big Mama was the backbone of the family and had a way of making all her family members feel special. She was blessed with love, grace, patience, understanding and forgiveness. She was also filled with wisdom and exemplified the true meaning of love. Big Mama had a strong love for both God and her fellow man. She frequently explained how the family's traditional Sunday dinners came about and why the delicacies were labeled "food for the soul." Big Mama also went on to explain that although times were hard in the past, the family had always trusted God and stood together and had somehow always made it through.

As the movie progresses, reality sets in. We witness a first-hand account of how things began to really fall apart. Everyone had issues. The return of cousin Faith caused mayhem. Lem had just been released from jail, and Teri and Miles' marriage was in a very bad place. Big Mama later fell ill and life as the family knew it began to unravel. The family that originally seemed to have it all together found themselves amidst a whirlwind of chaos.

Isn't it good to know that God works miracles? Isn't it good to know that when you are worn to your core and it seems as if all hope is gone, God's mercy appears from out of nowhere? Near the end of the movie and before the credits began to roll, each family member experienced a life lesson and was transformed by forgiveness, understanding, love or redemption. *Soul Food* brilliantly illustrates real-life situations, barriers and circumstances. It reminds us that as Christians, we should lay all judgments aside and embrace one another in love. Through prayer, faith, meditation and reflection, we are able to hear the voice of God, who longs for us to embrace one another in adversity. We are called to connect with the strength from within and strive to become an example of strong, yet compassionate Christians.

As Christians, we are faced with many circumstances in life that can cause "internal injuries," leading to a life of pain and sometimes resulting in permanent scars.

We live in a world that no longer seems to care. We sometimes feel as though we are fighting an uphill battle against the world. It makes you wonder if God has abandoned you. Moreover, the simple pleasures in life can seem unattainable, while the pains of life seem never-ending. Every time you've endured one storm, another tumultuous cloud is in the making. Each time you put out one fire, as it's smoldering, you find yet another spark that turns into a flame, and it is heading full-force in your direction. It seems to never end. It's always one thing after another.

How do you handle adversity? How do you respond to others who are facing trying times and rough spots in their personal lives? It may sound cliché, but love and understanding could make the world a far better place, a more peaceful place where it is a whole lot easier to get to where you are trying to go or be the person you are striving to be.

It is not my intent to sound preachy or self-righteous. That is far from what I hope to achieve. As you read this book, my only request is that you step into a broader scope of life's journey. Allow God to work through you and me as we embark upon a path that will lead us in the direction of peace and reconciliation. We are intrinsically bound to one another because our similarities are much greater than all of our differences. Please know that we all hurt. We all have fears and desire a shoulder to lean on, an ear to listen to us. I am not too proud to say that at one point or another, I have sorely needed someone's ear for listening or someone's shoulder to lean on during many adversities in my life.

Figuratively speaking, in order to maintain our spiritual health, our inner being requires hydration and nourishment. Many of us have our own way of handling adversity.

Some of us shed tears. Sometimes a simple smile is a plea for understanding. A tilt of the head is an outward sentiment for desired adoration. An outburst of laughter may actually be symbolic for saying, "If you only knew what I am going through right now . . ." Some of us sit alone quietly, which may be a sign that we simply want someone to offer a warm embrace. Sometimes, we may call a friend and say, "I need to talk." Ultimately, we opt for a whispered prayer to God with a simple request, "Lord, just give me peace."

Before I conclude, allow me to make one thing perfectly clear. This is not a pity party. This is not a license to hang your head in despair. No matter what you may be going through or no matter how you choose to get through your troubling times, this is an invitation to better understand why life's situations and disappointments are always knocking on our door. It is strictly up to us how we choose to answer. We can go directly to the door of distress, head-strong and steadfast, or we can just sit quietly as the doorbell continuously rings and passively listen in both apprehension and fear.

My poetry and words of inspiration were written from a combination of personal experiences and the experiences of others. I nicknamed the entries "snapshots" because sometimes it takes a snapshot to tell an entire story and other times a snapshot only represents part of a whole. At any rate it's all about being transparent. It's all about raw emotions and expressing feelings. It illustrates the fluctuation between being overwhelmed and about to throw in the towel and then thanking and praising God in the midst of everything you have been through or are currently going through. Overall, it is about life, love and everything in between. Take some time to read *"From Pain to Praise."*

Enjoy!

Open Letter

Greetings,

'm taking this opportunity to free myself from the effects of your actions, words and deception. Life's journey steers our travels across myriad people, places and situations. Some experiences are positive and nurturing, while other experiences can cloud the atmosphere.

I pray that someday you will take ownership for the negative atmosphere you created. I have always tried to extract the good in people, accepting them for who they are. I welcomed you into my personal space without reservation or judgment. I was unaware that from the onset, you had an agenda. Instead of requited friendship and open sincerity, your offering was self-absorption and the need for a nurtured ego. How unfortunate.

In order for me to move on and fully realize what God has in store for me, I had to ask Him to forgive me for how I felt about you after you revealed your true identity. You pretended to want the best for me, appearing to cheer me on in life, while all along you were hoping that I would self-destruct or simply fail.

I'm proud that I never populated your clique. I chose to be singly strong instead of collectively wrong. And to this day, you continue to live your life without remorse or conviction. I accept the revelation that I never should have allowed you to occupy that much space in my life any way.

We're human and we all fall short. But as Christians, at the very least, our plight should humble us. We should never be in a place where we hesitate to rectify our wrongs. Instead, we should be proponents for the virtues of humility and a kind and genuine spirit.

My offering of transparency in this letter is what makes this process so cathartic for me. I'm sure you've heard the phrase, *hurt people hurt people.* To the contrary, I would never want to hurt anyone inadvertently or purposely as a result of my experience with you.

Though you tried to curse me, I bless you. After all you've said and done, I would never want you to experience the pain I've endured.

God has instructed me to love my enemies and to forgive them. I refuse to miss out on my blessings because of you or anyone else.

I forgive you, and I am a better person for surviving the ride you orchestrated. I have full control of the wheel now, and my ride is a whole lot smoother than before. God has granted me the peace of mind I so longed for. I give Him the glory for allowing me to live, learn, grow, love, forgive and move on. And had it not been for the clouds or the rain, I would have never experienced the joy of His healing sunshine.

From the bottom of my heart, I wish you well.

Spiritually submitted,

Kathy

Snapshot:

> When everything seems to fall down upon you and when nothing seems right . . . Rest assured that each tear of distress merges into a river of strength that commands a smoother flow through the treacherous waters of life.

> ~Kathy M. Walters

We often wonder what to do during the "in-between" time and while we are "in the midst of it all." Sometimes, we have to stand still and allow God to do His perfect work. Sometimes, he is simply requesting our attention. We should learn to remain steadfast and focused no matter how complex or complicated life may seem.

PART 1

Don't Ever Stop Dreaming, Praying and Trying

God's Lemonade

No matter how many pitfalls you encounter in life, you must keep the momentum. No matter how many trials you face and no matter how many burdens you bear, you have to keep moving. Know that while God rains on the just as well as the unjust . . . He still reigns.

Life can really throw some curves at us. We have setbacks, letdowns, betrayals, you name it. Other times we may feel as though we want to just throw in the towel and give up. Life and all it has to offer will defy us into thinking that all hope is gone and our dreams will never come true. You pray and you try and then you try all over again. Nothing happens. Nothing moves. You've spoken into the atmosphere and written your vision. Still your dreams return void. You've kept the faith. You've prayed to God. Still nothing happens.

What do you do and where do you go from here? What happens next? Well . . . you turn to God; you dream, pray and try even harder. Dreams should never be shattered or forgotten.

We should never throw in the towel or give up or give in no matter how dark the clouds may seem. Always stay focused even when the dream-killers and prayer-stoppers navigate their way into your life.

There are times when we have to reevaluate our lives and our associations. Sometimes our negative thoughts are pure derivatives from an association with the wrong circle of people. Everyone that smiles and appears to be connected to you is not authentic. Unfortunately, we encounter individuals who have "strategically planned agendas." Consequently, we live in a world of manipulators and negative prognosticators. They are always looking and hoping for something negative to happen. Throughout life, you can be assured that you will encounter a plethora of individuals who are always manipulating a situation for the detriment of your peace of mind and for their own self-satisfaction.

This is an opportune time for the "enemy" to begin playing tricks with your mind. You begin to act out as a result of negative thoughts and intrusive impediments. Your faith is challenged. Your spirits are low. Your dreams may temporarily appear out of reach. Mayhem seems to have taken the controls as you move forward to navigate your way through your ordeal. But guess what? This has the potential to be a good thing. You might ask, *"A good thing? How could that be?"* Well, haven't you heard the old adage about turning lemons into lemonade?

One lesson I've learned is that how we deal with the challenges and the blows that life has to offer lies within the palm of our hands. It is a decision. Yes, a decision. We ultimately choose whether or not we want to be happy. We choose whether or not we will allow life's struggles or the naysayers' comments to keep us down. We choose to transform the negative to inner joy, peace and a renewed outlook on life. We choose to seek for the wisdom needed to move on in life.

I found great inspiration in a woman named Janie. My heart went out to her. When I first met Janie, she was disheveled because she had recently gone through a divorce, unfairly lost her job and her mortgage company had begun foreclosure proceedings. She was so open and honest and often revealed so much of what she was going through. She discussed her daughter, Lola and the challenges she now face as a single mom. Janie was nearly in tears as she shared detailed accounts of how her life had practically changed overnight. I felt badly for Janie because she was such a warm and kind person. She asked if we could pray together, and we did. We also agreed that the next time we saw each other things would be better.

Janie came by my office a few weeks later. She didn't call ahead of time, so I wasn't expecting her. She sat across from my desk with a huge smile on her face. She was glowing. I knew something spectacular must have taken place. I knew God had blessed her with something really special. I asked Janie if she'd found a job.

"No."

"Did your ex-husband finally forward the retroactive child support payments?"

"No."

"Oh. Did your lender stop the foreclosure proceedings?"

"No."

"Well, tell me what happened!" I finally said to her. "The suspense is driving me crazy."

Janie simply told me that God had spoken to her in a mighty way through her child. Janie explained that her daughter walked up to her one day as she was job searching on her laptop.

Lola smiled saying "Mommy, I love you so much. I'm glad you love me more, too."

Janie gazed at Lola with a perplexed look. "Lola, honey what do you mean?" "I have always loved you and I . . ." Lola quickly interrupted.

"Mommy, you spend so much more time with me now. You aren't angry when you come home from work and we are always doing things together. I'm so glad God took your job from you."

Janie never realized it before, but it was now revealed how stressed and entangled she had been with her career. She was sad to find that until recently, quality time with Lola had been non-existent. Lola had never said a word or in any way indicated to Janie how she felt. Janie immediately apologized to Lola and told her how sorry she was.

Lola told her that apologies weren't necessary because God had already begun pouring lemonade. Janie, once again puzzled, looked at Lola and inquired, "Little girl, what are you talking about?"

"Okay, Mommy. I will tell you exactly what happened."

One night I was trying to fall asleep so that I could dream of you spending more time with me, and it began to rain. I remembered an activity my Sunday school teacher shared with us. The topic was: "When life serves you lemons, make lemonade."

Well, I jumped out of bed and ran over to my play area. I knew if I went into the kitchen, you would hear me, so I changed my plan. I removed a pair of scissors from my supply box, sorted through my construction paper and removed all the yellow sheets. I began cutting out lemon shapes. I grabbed a pitcher and a writing pen, and wrote something on each lemon. *My mommy is not happy. My mommy is never at the bus stop. My mommy is always on her laptop. My mommy works too late.* I thought real hard as I wrote on the last lemon. I wanted to save the best for last. *God, please take my mommy's job away.*

Lola prayed as she placed each lemon in the pitcher. She then set the pitcher on the side of her bed as she listened to the rain fall. Lola had another idea. She opened her window and allowed the raindrops to fall into the pitcher. *God, I don't ask for much. I never complain. I try my best to be a good girl. I love my mommy and I want her to spend more time with me and love me more. God, I dream of the day when my dreams will come true. I am going to keep praying and trying until something happens. If you don't do it right now, I am going to dream, pray and try again. God, please make these lemons into lemonade.*

By then, Janie and I both were in tears as she told me what brought her into my office that day. I couldn't believe a little girl could have such gown-up "faith." Now I knew why Janie's entire demeanor had changed and I also knew the source of the glow.

God's gifts come in different forms and in mysterious ways. As a child, Lola wanted God to take her mother's job away. From Lola's vantage point, finances weren't an issue. She just wanted her mother's attention. Here lies a phenomenal story.

Janie was a prayer warrior. She constantly prayed that God would turn her situation around. Though down at times, Janie remained steadfast. She, too, never gave up, and fortunately, her story has a happy ending.

Janie's ex-husband miraculously repaid everything he owed and brought his child support payments up to date. Janie found the job she'd been praying for. She is now working from the comfort of her own home, setting her own schedule. And can I mention that her salary more than doubled? Janie's top priority was spending as much time as possible with Lola and waiting for her at the bus stop every single day. They are at bible study each week and at early service on

Sundays. The household is now filled with much love and quality time spent with one another.

Things were not easy in the beginning. Everything seemed dim for both Janie and Lola. Each had their own way of crying out to God. We must learn to step back so that God can take control. God works in His own time, and in His own way. Our only charge is to keep trusting and believing. God is the substance that turns the sour into sweet and the impossible into possible. Before you know it, you will begin thanking Him for the lemons in your life. No matter what you're going through, keep the faith. The pain can sometimes be unbearable, but don't give up. Don't ever stop dreaming, praying and trying. God has lemonade waiting just for you!

Snapshot:

Everyone possesses a license for
healing, harvesting and redemp-
tion. That license never expires.

~Kathy M. Walters

 ave you ever struggled in life? Have you ever thought your situation seemed hopeless or your dreams were out of reach? This is the time when you turn it over to God, give praise to Him, be grateful for the journey, and look forward to the overflow of blessings.

PART 2

Bradford

radford's expression was one of perplexity as he gazed into the mirror. He stared at himself in total disbelief over how his life had changed in the blink of an eye. Just three months before, his life was great. He had just received promotion number two within a year and had moved into his dream home. His daughter, Brie, was happy and healthy and there was only one missing link in his quest toward total happiness.

Out of the clear blue sky, Bradford's wife, Melanie, told him that she had something really important to discuss. Bradford was ecstatic. He knew Melanie was going to announce that there was going to be an addition to their family. They had often talked about having more children so that Brie wouldn't grow up alone. Family was important to Bradford. He had two brothers and a younger sister. They were very close and he wanted to encourage the same closeness with his own children. Bradford loved children and he relished the idea of having as many as possible. *The more the merrier*, he often thought.

To Bradford's dismay, his speculation about what was on Melanie's mind couldn't have been further from his dreams. Melanie's revelation to Bradford was plain and simple. She'd rather be free than "miserably tied down as a wife and mother." She felt Bradford was "too settled" and didn't know how to live life on the edge. *Shouldn't all married men be settled?* he thought. His party days were over and his first priority was his family.

Bradford was a faithful husband and provided Melanie and Brie with the best of what life had to offer. He spent quality time with his "favorite girls," they enjoyed family vacations abroad, and he was always there when either of them needed him. He attended to their slightest beckoning call. But once Bradford heard the big announcement, he realized his love was simply not enough.

There was no question about the custody of Brie. Sadly, Melanie told Bradford that Brie could "stay" with him because she wouldn't have time to "watch her." Bradford's mantra was that he was willing to give a lifetime of love, but he couldn't spend one moment in love as a fool. Although he loved Melanie dearly, he would not try to hold her to a marriage that she described as "getting on her nerves." He would not put up a fight. He would simply let her go.

He soon found out that Melanie was both cruel and calculating. She already had her bags packed and loaded in the trunk of the car. Her second announcement was that she was on her way to the beautiful condo she has been renting downtown for the past six months!

Brie was the apple of Bradford's eye, and he hated to see his baby girl saddened by Melanie's lack of affection towards her own family. Bradford never wanted to see his marriage dissolve, but deep down inside, he had known that something wasn't right for some time now. Melanie had become so detached. From the outside, they were the perfect family. At church, so many people admired the Carters. They were regarded as the epitome of happiness. It's funny how things appear differently when you are looking in from the outside.

It was late on a Friday afternoon, not long after Melanie's announcement, when Dr. Berman removed his glasses, looked Bradford straight in the eyes, and told him that he had prostate cancer. Bradford felt as if all of the air had been sucked out of the room. Other than more frequent restroom visits, Bradford didn't feel any differently and hadn't noticed any other symptoms.

Bradford immediately invited his family over. He knew he had to tell everyone what was happening. Many would have crumbled under the weight of a dissolving marriage, the prospect of raising a child alone, and now, a diagnosis of cancer. But, Bradford knew he serves a God who is awesome and who would never abandon him, no matter what.

Bradford's thoughts as he gazed into the mirror were interrupted when he heard his sister, Gloria tap on the bathroom door.

"Bradford, are you ready, honey? It's time for us to head out."

"Okay, G. I'm coming. Give me a sec."

Bradford loved his sister. He loved all of his siblings, but Gloria had a special place in his heart. She was the youngest of four, and Bradford felt he had to take care of her. They were only 18 months apart, so they practically grew up as twins.

After hearing of her brother's cancer, Gloria knew she would do everything possible to make sure that he had the best care while she remained steadfastly by his side.

Both Gloria and Bradford had built a rapport with staff members and other cancer patients during Bradford's visits to the doctor. There was one lovely couple, Jamila and Todd, who stood out. They were both so fond of this devoted couple. Ironically, Bradford and Todd's radiation treatment times coincided, so the foursome had some great conversations in the lobby area.

Gloria was so close to Bradford that sometimes she could feel his pain. She would often wake up in the middle of the night and begin to pray for him. They had a strong connection. Sometimes they would finish each other's sentences or know what the other was thinking. The mere thought of no longer having her brother in her life brought Gloria to tears. Gloria knew that she had to be strong for Bradford and continue to pray, trust and believe in God's word, but sometimes she became weak. She felt as though Bradford was already dealing with a broken heart, and now this. She prayed that he would remain strong.

One day, while at the doctor's office, Bradford reached over and placed his hand on top of his sister's and smiled. She just looked at him and said, "I know. Everything is going to be alright." He said, "Everything is going to be fine. We're going to get through this. Don't worry, sis."

Dr. Berman explained the various symptoms and side effects of treatment. Bradford had heard so many stories about men becoming sterile after prostate cancer, and this was the fear that haunted him the most. He prayed:

Lord,

I know that you are the one and only God. You are the awesome God who has healed and performed miracles in the past and you are still healing and performing miracles right now. My faith and trust lay solely in you. I am thanking you in advance for healing me and preserving my ability to become a father once again. Amen.

In addition, Dr. Berman explained that the treatment for prostate cancer had advanced quite a bit within the past few years. Since Bradford's cancer was detected in the early stages, there was no reason why he shouldn't have a speedy recovery and lead a normal life. "As a matter of fact," Dr. Berman chimed, "In a few months' time, this will seem as if it never happened."

It had been six months since Bradford's last round of radiation treatments. Occasionally, Gloria would spend the night to be there for Brie and Bradford. Bradford kept telling Gloria that he was patient, prayerful and unmovable in his faith. Bradford shared with Gloria that he was aware when she would come into his room and watch quietly as he would cradle his face in his hands. He explained that those moments were his praise and worship time. There were times when he would worship and praise God all night long, whether it was in his bedroom, the bathroom or any other room in the house. Sometimes, he would praise God during radiation. When Gloria thought he was at his lowest point, he was actually engaged in praise.

One Friday evening, Bradford, Brie, Gloria and Todd were out for a celebratory dinner at Istanblue restaurant in the Buckhead district of Atlanta. A post-treatment appointment determined that Bradford was cancer—free. Everyone was so thankful and grateful and knew of no better way to celebrate than going to Bradford's favorite restaurant. After the food was served, everyone held hands as Bradford blessed the food:

Lord, we are coming to you with thankful hearts. We have so much to be thankful for, and we know that where we are and how we made it through are solely due to your grace and mercy. We ask that you grant us with a mind determined to do your will and that we continue to walk in the path you would have

chosen for us. We ask that you bless this food for the nourish-
ment of our bodies and we honor you with our undying praise.
In Jesus' name, Amen.

As they began to eat, they suddenly heard a voice out of nowhere call out, "I am so sorry I'm late." Gloria immediately stood with a huge smile on her face. Bradford was taken aback as he saw Jamila, but he was pleasantly surprised. Gloria asked the server to bring another chair and she then hurried over to embrace Jamila.

Whenever Bradford, Gloria, Jamila and Todd talked, they would discuss the treatments, events in the news, weather, sports and anything else that came to mind.

It wasn't until a few days ago when Gloria saw Jamila, Todd and Todd's fiancée Audrey, grocery shopping at a Kroger grocery store that she found out Jamila and Todd were brother and sister! Jamila was single and available. Todd and Jamila were fraternal twins and their extended family lived in Washington, D.C. When Bradford, Gloria, Jamila and Todd were together, they never discussed how they were related. Each assumed that the other were husband and wife. What a wonderful surprise! Gloria immediately asked for Jamila's phone number and invited her to have dinner with them.

Gloria explained everything to Bradford and he was ecstatic. The rest is history. Since that dinner, Bradford and Jamila recapped conversations they had at the doctor's office. They reminisced about how they enjoyed one another, but since each thought the other was married, they merely thought God had placed them in each other's paths simply to make Bradford and Todd's treatment a bit easier.

Today, Bradford and Jamila are basking in joy and are head over heels in love. They are dating exclusively, and Brie absolutely loves Jamila. Bradford has already purchased a ring for Jamila and is planning his proposal to her. Jamila longs to have children, and she loves Brie unconditionally. Bradford knows that he will finally have the family he has always desired. Dr. Berman confirmed that fact a month ago. Bradford was excited about discovering the right time to propose to Jamila and make her his wife and the mother of his children. He still believes in love. And, in addition to Gloria and his mom, his desire is to have another positive female figure in his daughter's life. Bradford strongly believes that God knows our heart's desires. He also feels that once he has prayed to God for something, he should leave it alone, let go and let God. That's exactly what he did.

Bradford sat in the den watching the Atlanta Falcon vs. the New Orleans Saints. He could overhear Jamila and Brie in the kitchen, planning Brie's seventh birthday party. He turned down the volume and listened in amusement to their upcoming plans. Bradford couldn't help but thank and praise God for restoring his health and fulfilling his life. He was happier than he had been in a long time. He wouldn't change any part of his journey over the past year and a half. It was a resounding confirmation that "all things work together for good to them that love God." Bradford can only imagine the joy that his future holds, because more than anything, he knows who holds the future. Indeed, we serve an awesome God!

Snapshot:

Your tribulations are merely triumphs placed on "pause."

~Kathy M. Walters

There is no greater gift than the gift of life. Placing pen to paper was my only way of expressing my feelings after witnessing the birth of my sister's first—born. Unfortunately, he was already an angel when he entered this world.

Although it was a very difficult time for my sister, her husband and the rest of the family, we all know that God is still in control.

For any woman who has lost a baby, our hearts are with you. My sister was extremely generous and gracious enough to share her experience in her own words below. I wrote and wish to dedicate the poem that follows my sister's story to our "unforgotten angels." We love you!

PART 3

In Her Own Words . . .

I know that it all really happened but at times it's a blur, almost as if it was in another lifetime or either like it happened to someone else and not me. I remember having this weird feeling in my stomach and lower region. I dismissed it for a couple of days and then finally decided to call the doctor's office. I left two messages with the nurse, but neither she nor the doctor ever called me back. This was my first pregnancy and little did I know that these weird feelings I was having were contractions.

The next thing I knew, I felt a gush of water. My husband said he'd never heard me run up the 14 steps in our house so fast in all the years we'd been married. The water was still rushing down my legs. He called my sister, who's a nurse . . . neither of us perhaps realizing what was really going on. He called 9-1-1 and then my mother. The water was still rushing down my legs. There I lay on the bathroom floor in the fetal position, holding myself and screaming for my baby boy's life.

The paramedics got me on the stretcher and proceeded to take me down those same 14 stairs I'd sprinted up minutes before. Once inside the ambulance, one of the medics asked if he could pray for me and my baby. His sincerity touched me in such a way that I will never forget. I welcomed his prayer.

At the hospital, it seemed as if it took forever for the doctor to come in and check on me. My baby needed every precious minute. The ultrasound showed that there was no more amniotic fluid to protect my son and no way for him to survive. There was no movement. He was gone. Gone to heaven. I couldn't believe it. This was NOT happening to me.

All the dreams and hopes I had for his future were gone in a flash. The onesies I'd purchased were hanging in his closet. What in the world did I do to cause this to happen? I was eating right. I got enough sleep. How could I be SO STUPID to not know that I was having contractions? What if the doctor's office had called me back like they were supposed to? What if I had gone to the emergency room earlier in the day? What if?

So tiny, so perfect. Ten little toes and ten little fingers. Perfect facial features. Unbelievable. There he was wrapped in a tiny hand-sewn gown and a matching little hat. I'll cherish and keep them both as long as I live.

Mommy loves you, and will see you again.

A Tribute to the Miller Angels

A Face to Behold, But Eyes to Yet See

How was I to have ever known
That on that special day we'd meet
Your face I would forever behold
But your eyes, I would never see
I had imagined your little precious smile
And the softness of your touch
That overwhelming angelic tenderness
Of loving you so much
A brand new life
Beautiful bright eyes
A gift filled with mountains of joy
But the unmatched joy
Your parents had to have felt
When they were told they were having a boy
That transformation
Of a love so strong
To a heart-wrenching pain so deep
You departed before you truly arrived
You meant the world to me
Not one spoken word
But, a bond we shared
Because I know
That you know
That I
Was there
Holding you close
For as long as I could
I kept crying," This isn't so!"
I rocked you
I gazed at you
I prayed to God for you
I couldn't

Just let
You go
Without giving you a smile
The indelible truth
I will love you forever more
I graced you with a kiss
And called you my "Sweetheart"
For my heart
Was truly torn
So much to tell you
So much for you to know
This is so unfair, you see
Inconceivably taken
This tiny soul
With you, goes a part of me
Through hope and prayer I'll make it through
I often still shed tears
For tears are shed
To purify the soul
Making the windows of life more clear
So I have a new perspective
As I now look back
To the day
Your soul was set free
I shed less tears
Our bond, eternally sealed
For I know, one day
Your eyes, I will see!

Update:

Through God's undeniable grace and continuous mercy, the Millers are now the proud parents of two beautiful boys. They are happy and healthy! We couldn't have asked for anything better. God is awesome!

Snapshot:

When pain seems to paralyze your soul, the praise will pull you through.

~ Kathy M. Walters

We often hear the phrase, "You never know what the person sitting next to you is going through." What a powerful statement! Life brings both the expected and the unexpected. Life's journey will teach us to grasp hope in spite of what appears to be a hopeless situation.

PART 4

My Pen, My Paper, My Heart . . . My Story

had a very happy childhood. My home was filled with an abundance of love and laughter. My parents, still the most beautiful people I know, made sure the household ran smoothly and my siblings and I had everything we needed. My parents always communicated, laughed and talked to us and we were always going somewhere or doing something fun.

Our extended family would always get together every weekend. Whether there was a holiday or not, the family would gather merely for the sake of being together. We always had a great time.

Both of my grandmothers, Lizzie and Emily along with my great grandmother, Clifford, whom we called Mother Dear, were a huge link in the family ties. I attribute my love and high regard for family to the solid foundation that I was blessed with from the moment I was born. Life for me couldn't have been any better!

I had many friends in my neighborhood. I can remember teaching Science, Math and Social Studies to the older kids who lived nearby. Yes, the older kids. They would excitedly show up at my doorstep with notebooks and pencils in hand. They would give me their undivided attention during class, and they would hold their stomachs laughing when I would tell funny stories or explain why frogs hopped.

I "taught class" for what seemed like hours, especially during the summer months. Some of my students would wait for me on my steps until I came outside. At twelve o'clock sharp each day, I would leave my class and go in the house for lunch. My mother prepared the coolest lunches. Whenever I had a sandwich, it would be cut into the cutest little shapes and placed on my favorite pink plate. I usually drank water or occasionally some cherry Kool-Aid since I hated milk and juice. For dessert, I had two butter cookies. Every day, I wore two little gold rings that my mother bought me. I also wore three gold bangles on my right arm that I had asked my dad to buy. I loved jewelry early on. I still do. And for some reason, when I placed the two butter cookies on my fingers, I felt that was the true symbol which reflected my wealth as a teacher. Without fail, I would resume my lecture right after lunch, picking up where I left off.

To this day, it tickles me to think back on how my neighbors gravitated toward my humor and zeal for life. At the time, I wasn't even old enough to be teaching on the academic level I was allegedly teaching. The majority of my material was incorrect, I'm sure.

Okay, so I was in kindergarten and my students ranged from first through third grade. Go figure. I loved being in the spotlight and they were a great audience. Hey, if they were okay with it, so was I. I loved words. I loved writing. I loved hearing myself talk. I would sit around the dinner table with my family and create interesting topics for discussion. I would make up a song or a speech at the drop of a hat.

I remember being so happy one evening as we were riding in the car on our way home from yet another family function. I was in the back seat with my oldest sister, and my parents were up front. I began singing and rhyming. I was proud to try out a new set of "big" words I'd learned. Everyone in the car was laughing, and I was overjoyed because more than anything, I loved to make my family laugh. I loved performing. I would wiggle my head and neck as I gestured with my little hands when I spoke. As the adrenaline flowed from the momentum of being in the spotlight, I immediately thought of some additional material and rhymed my little behind off! All of the sudden without warning, the car became quiet. You could have heard a fly peeing on a cotton ball! My parents looked at one other in total shock and my father nearly swerved the car to a screeching halt! I can remember Mom and Dad immediately and simultaneously lecturing me. I was totally oblivious to what had just occurred. I was on a roll. The rhyme sounded great and I was offended that I had been interrupted mid-performance. How was I supposed to know that one of my latest "big words" would change the atmosphere? I only used a word that I thought rhymed with constitution . . . I have no idea where I'd heard the word or even what it meant. I just knew it rhymed. How was I supposed to know that *prostitution* was a bad word?! I was only five years old! Needless to say, after my parents explained why I shouldn't use that word, my entertainment session abruptly ended. I immediately retreated as I stared out the car window and began observing the night life. I was mesmerized by the array of colors beaming from everywhere. I began to gaze at the brake lights from the back of all the stopped and slowing cars, and then I focused on the street lights and the skyline of Atlanta. I reluctantly looked over at my older sister, who had remained quiet during the entire lecture.

Instantly, I felt better as she displayed a soft, loving smile showing the biggest, prettiest dimples I'd ever seen. I sheepishly smiled in return and slid back in the seat of the car. I rode the rest of the way home without saying another word.

The next morning, I woke up happy, rejuvenated and ready to start my day. It's amazing how resilient children can be. I walked into the kitchen, kissed my parents, ate my breakfast and sang all the way out the door. The day was Saturday, my day off. No Science, no Math, no Social Studies, no students. All I wanted to do was go outside and be a kid.

As time progressed, my family life was still as awesome as ever. I'd maintained a close circle of friends and I was always surrounded by people who had my best interests at heart. I was in love with life. But then, life happened.

Suddenly, my entire world changed. Something was different. Life seemed to take an abrupt and devastating turn.

From out of nowhere, I began having unexplained episodes of anxiety and panic attacks. Without warning, the attacks would emerge and take complete control of me. My heart would beat so rapidly that I could see the rhythm of my heartbeat through my clothing and

I could hear pounding in my eardrums. My heart pounded to one rhythm while my ears pounded to another. I was amazed at how one organ in my body could become a symphony and create beats in two different places, producing dismal melodies that only I could hear.

My chest seemed to cave in as I struggled with shortness of breath. Each gasp would create an overwhelming sense of fear. Every sensation of what I was feeling escalated. Frantic, I would try to hold onto anything nearby for stability. I would tremble uncontrollably with fear and my eyes would well with tears, blurring my vision.

Sometimes the tears wouldn't fall. They would just sit there as if they, too, were afraid to face the world. I was beyond being comforted. *God, why is this happening to me? Please help me.*

One Sunday morning, when I was on my way to church, an attack erupted. I was on I—20 westbound near Langhorn Street and Martin Luther King Jr. Drive. While listening to the radio and taking in the sights on and around the interstate, I began to tremble. I felt the onset of yet another panic attack. *Not now, God. Please, not now.* My throat became extremely dry, and the palpitations began. I wanted to pull over, but somehow I felt that it was best to keep driving. I was driving as fast as my heart was beating.

The more fearful I became, the faster I drove. I needed to call someone. Anyone. I was trembling beyond control as I reached for my cell phone. I picked it up, but I lost my grasp and it slipped out of my hand and onto the floor of the car. I then gripped the steering wheel and held on so tightly that the palm of my hands began to turn beet red. It seemed as though the trees, cars and everything I observed before were now closing in on me.

※ ※ ※

By the time I made it to the church parking lot, I was a nervous wreck. I was sweating and trembling, my heart was still beating rapidly and the symphony was still performing within my body. I exited my car as quickly as I could. I'd managed to retrieve my cell phone and purse and begin my journey towards the church doors. A few feet seemed like miles by the time I made it to the entryway. As soon as I reached for the door, a gentleman was walking out. Somehow, I made it past him without collapsing then and there. *God, please help me!*

I know that it was through divine intervention that my eyes locked onto three of my favorite church members, Gail Warren, Barbara L. Arline and Mother Marion W. Ward. They were all standing in the vestibule. I have no idea which of them embraced me first, but I'd never been happier to see these three ladies in my entire life.

They each had warm smiles as usual, and we greeted one another with hugs, but they had no idea what I was going through at the time. I tried to smile and pretend that everything was okay. But it definitely wasn't. The dissonant beats within my body had progressed to another verse, and the demeanor I portrayed on the outside was in stark contrast to the turmoil I was enduring on the inside. With each hug, I held on for dear life. I just knew that Gail or Barbara or Mother Ward would be able to feel the strong, rapid beat of my heart and the trembling throughout my body. But fortunately, they never noticed. I believe their warmth and sincerity was the catalyst through which God comforted me. Until they read this book, they had been totally oblivious to the indelible mark they made on my life that day. They had no idea how they had helped to calm my storm. And I am so grateful that on that day, Gail Warren, Barbara L. Arline, and Mother Marion W. Ward were my God—sent angels. Humble, sincere and totally unknowing. Thank God for angels.

There was no specific time when the attacks would occur, so I was always fearful and on edge. I prayed that God would provide me with something, anything that would take my mind off "me" and everything I was going through. I wanted my life back. I was living a nightmare. Life and what I used to recognize as living had taken on new meaning. I was over-shadowed by a mighty demon that I couldn't seem to conquer. I would like to say that my life was like a roller coaster. But even roller coasters have both ups and downs. If I could have had one good day in a given month, I would have been ecstatic.

As days, weeks and months passed, I continued to keep my deep, dark secret. I can recall so many holidays when I was surrounded by fifty or more people in a room. They would be laughing, talking and having a good time. Though I was in the midst of a jubilant atmosphere, I felt as if I was alone and the only person in the world. These were the people who were closest to me, yet I was disconnected. Neither the funniest joke nor the warmest smile could disengage me from feeling isolated, lonely and sad. The joy and peace I used to cherish was now stripped from the core of everything that defined me. I had no more dreams, goals or aspirations. I felt that no amount of love or laughter could fill the void that followed every breath I took. I was now suffering from depression.

Anxiety, panic attacks and now depression. I was worn. Every time I endured one storm, another tumultuous cloud was in the making. I never could have foreseen what happened next.

One Friday morning, a dear friend of mine asked me to meet her for lunch. We both had only an hour and a half, so we knew we had to move quickly in order to eat, catch up on girl talk and make it back to our respective offices. We talked, laughed and had a great time. At one point, she displayed a serious look on her face, paused and asked me if everything was okay. I told her that everything was not okay, but when time permitted, we could sit down and discuss everything that was going on. She always knew when something was bothering me and I could always detect when things weren't going well in her life. We always confided in one another, and normally we would have done so on that day. But for some strange reason that particular day just didn't seem like the best time. I couldn't bring myself to tell her what was wrong. Lunch ended, and we talked about how much we enjoyed hanging out and having fun.

We were disappointed because time flew by quickly and we would have loved to have had more time. We hugged and said our goodbyes. When I returned to my office, she called and asked me if I was sure I didn't want to tell her what was bothering me. We laughed about it and agreed that we would get together and talk in two days.

Unfortunately, two days never came because she passed away the next morning.

My story includes additional snapshots from experiences in my life. I lost my great-grandmother, both of my grandmothers, a favorite aunt, a favorite uncle and many other loved ones. As a child, I was bullied by an adult.

I survived a tornado, and I nearly drowned at the neighborhood pool. As an adult, I had to make a career change, which resulted in starting over from scratch. I lived with low-self esteem. A trusted business partner stole money from me. I had dreams that failed, and friends who turned their backs on me. I suffered an injury that resulted in daily physical therapy for a year. I was hurt by "church folk." I made it through four surgeries within two years. I endured months of speech therapy, learning breathing techniques and re-learning to enunciate words, praying that I would regain my speech. Like so many of us, I have been talked about. I have been misunderstood and mis-construed. There were times when I simply didn't have any fight left to defend myself because I was caught between trying to do what was right and handling things on my own, as if God needed my help.

And the list goes on and on . . . Just as I had done with the anxiety and panic attacks, I was determined to keep the depression a secret as well. So I began praying even harder, asking God to heal me. I can't recall a single day or night that I didn't shed tears. I carried my bible everywhere, and I cradled it to my chest every night. I longed for a way out. I longed to have my old life back. I was emotionally and spiritually depleted. In my mind, I could imagine God becoming tired of my constant conversations with Him. My faith often wavered. I was in such spiritual warfare that there were times when I doubted God. There were times when I questioned Him. There were times when I was angry, and there were times when I just couldn't see my way through. *Why is this happening to me?* I often asked.

By the grace of God, I have a praise report. I've written about my resilience as a child. As an adult, resilience can be a challenge. I haven't always been able to bounce back right away, but God never failed me. Just when I was about to "cancel Christmas," He would always show up on Christmas Eve and make everything alright. I haven't always made the best decisions, but with each wrong decision, there was definitely a lesson learned from my mistake.

Through it all, I want everyone to know that life happens. We all are faced with trials and tribulations. I know that there are some who may read my story and find that it is just a speckle of what they have been through. And I respect that.

We each have our personalized storms and personalized stories. This happens to be mine. My charge is to share my storm and hopefully inspire and encourage others. No matter what I was going through, I stood firm in the hope that the Word of God would sustain and protect me. It had to. And I always maintained a direct line of communication with God. I never stopped praying to Him and I never stopped talking to Him. In the back of my mind, I knew that the only option I had was to simply wait on Him. And that I did. I prayed and I waited. I knew that He was my source and my refuge. I met with a counselor; I saw my primary care physician and I even took medication to control my panic attacks for a while. All of the above were fine, but their success was short—lived. Nothing or no one could do me like Jesus!

One day after months and months of praying, waiting and believing, I suddenly felt different. Halfway through that day, I paused and looked around. I placed my hand on my chest and realized that I actually felt good. Tears came to my eyes. Not from fear or panic this time, these were tears of joy. I wasn't nervous, trembling, or depressed. *Thank you, Jesus!* I actually felt good! I felt better than good! I went home that night and slept like a baby.

Weeks passed, and I realized that the sad beats which used to fill my eardrums and chest were replaced with a sense of joy. *Thank you, Jesus!* Joy was the only emotion now radiating throughout my body! God evicted that spirit of depression, and it no longer resides within me! *Praise God!*

To this day, I never use the word "depressed" to describe how I am feeling. For me, depression is a term that no longer exists. Occasionally, I still suffer from the panic and anxiety attacks, but these are much less frequent than before. And for that, I am truly grateful. If God can deliver me from one, I know He can deliver me from them all. I'll just wait. Without fail, I am still praying and standing on God's word. I know that my breakthrough is on the way.

For every tear, there's a triumph, for all sadness, there's a Savior, for every fall, there is Favor and for your dark place, there is Grace. I thank God for every tear, every mountain and every sorrow and affliction I have endured.

Sincerely,
My Pen, My Paper, My Heart . . . "My Story."

PART 5

Cathartic Creations: The poetic cleanse

Freestyle

Haiku

&

Poetic Expressions

Come in from the cold
His covering will warm you
His peace sustain you

You can keep your stamp
Only God validates me
Only stamp I need

Wow life is so good
Better now that God's within
Best time of my life

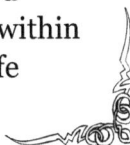

Love knows no reward
Like the prize I found in you
I am your prize too

Snapshot:

Through every dark cloud, trial, tribulation: God will always pull you through.

~Kathy M. Walters

Written in first person, this poem utilizes poignant expressions, metaphors, symbolism and hyperbole to reveal the anguish of someone who is in a very dark place. The greater message is clear: No matter how dim your circumstances or how grim your future may seem, God, in His infinite wisdom will always show up at the perfect time and He will definitely pull you through!

Outcry

God, are you listening?

For weeks, I would lie awake
        at night
        Alone
In the sheer of darkness
Tears staining pillows
that used to house the most pleasant
and peaceful dreams
Spirits staring and lurking
in the corridors
Slumber disturbed
by an unknown force of intention
I'm defeated
Lost in an undefined realm
of destruction
Hopes and dreams
now diminished
to a miniscule of nothing

Mind halted,
thus suspended
in a state of fear
Transformed,
transfixed,
transposed
How did I get here?
Sentenced to a lifetime
of catastrophic
imprisonment
Emotionally incarcerated
for the sake
of a generational curse
I had nothing to do with
Can't hear,
can't move,
can't groove
To the sweet,
sweet,
sound of the joy resonating
from what used to be
the tune of contentment
Rocking myself to sleep
through a self-serving lullaby
Just a worn down soul
in need
of just an outcry
Tell me,
how did I get here?
Trapped in this cold,
cold world
beyond measure
Inches,
feet,
miles,
eons of voided, unattainable,
yet so desired
pleasure

Feeling perplexed,
even sometimes vexed
Don't even want to discuss
the subject
Tell me, what's going on?
Every time I turn around,
reverberating sounds
Unadulterated,
unequivocal mishaps
Just trying to find my way
Yet accosted,
accused,
judged
shackled
and sentenced again in the same day
I'm worn
Bewildered
by this tainted source of treatment
A 360 degree circular circumference
of a volatile displacement
So down sometimes,
feeling like the orphan
of some reject
Tell me,
how did I get here?
Leverage lost
in an abyss of listlessness
Losing ground sometimes,
I cry out,
helpless
To my God I pray to
sometimes
I get so weary and restless
Never—ending screams
Unmanifested dreams
God, tell me please . . .
Are you listening?
Then, just when I

am about to lose hope
Peace comes over me
Confusion, now an illusion
Doubt is the enemy's intrusion
As I recapitulate
on just how good my God has been
You see,
through every dark cloud,
trial,
tribulation
God has always pulled me through
And by the grace of God
I can truly say
That if you ask Him
If you trust in Him
If you believe in Him
If you give it over to Him
He will create miracles for you!
No more outcry!

Snapshot:

> Given any increment of space or
> time, I will always ask for one
> more.

~Kathy M. Walters

Relationships can be quite complicated. They will either flourish or fade away in time.
Communication is very important between a husband and wife. In addition to the many other reasons marriages fail, failure to talk to one another can be detrimental.

The verbalization of feelings leaves less room for that which can destroy a relationship. The verbalization of feelings leaves less room for doubt and misunderstandings. The verbalization of feelings is not just for "you" but for both parties. It is the essence of give and take. This poem screams "real talk." It's not all about me. We are in this together. I will go the distance for you. I will be there for you. I need to know how you feel . . . just Talk to Me.

Talk to Me

Talk to me
Tell me how your day was
In more than just 1 sentence, 14 letters and 3 words
Just another day
Look at me
Not through the carnal eyes of a mere mortal
But through spiritual windows
Captivating my soul
And ultimately witnessing where only God dwells
Touch me
Not physically, within the first 4 –few seconds of being near me
But touch me
Within that inner-most, emotional crevice
Where no one has ever touched me before
Respect me
Knowing that I just can't settle for anything
But the respect you have for me
Causes you
To go above, about, beyond, beneath, beside, between
Anything that challenges you to do otherwise
Realizing that I am that quintessential queen
You are that qualitative king
As I abide in God, He abides in me
He illustrates
I appreciate
The total man He created you to be
You see, it's not all about me
I will travel across 8 continents

Hearing your name in 5 different languages
Being in love with you 366 days a year, 8 days a week, 25 hours a day,
    61 seconds a minute
Because given any increment of time or space

I will always ask for 1 more
I've told you countless, numerous times before
Talk to me
Tell me how your day was in more than just 1 sentence, 14 letters and
    3 little words
'Cause baby, it's never just another day!

Snapshot:

> Every pedestal wasn't placed
> merely to stand upon.
>
> ~ Kathy M. Walters

Can you recall a time when you felt loved and adored? The world seemed to be in the palm of your hands and everything in life was fantastic. You had close friends who you thought would never do you harm. Something happens. The friendship takes a turn. The ones who loved you so much suddenly turn their backs on you. Why did they place you on a pedestal only to tear you down for the whole world to see? Now it seems as if all eyes are on you.

Lifted, and Then Let Go

Her words are somewhat silenced
Her tears are suddenly few
Her heart is beyond broken
Her soul reflects the color of blue
No longer stemmed by emotion
Yet captured by the cold
Anesthetized and in a lonely place
The darkness now unfolds
Not a spark of light descending
No focus to make things clear
Prayers vanish once relinquished from her lips
Obliterated upon dispel
On top of the world unending
Ensconced so all will know
A poster child for failure and defeat
Lifted and then let go

Snapshot:

Don't allow your pillow to house
your tears anymore.

~ Kathy M. Walters

Have you ever been in an unproductive relationship? One that starts out fine and slowly goes down the drain? Have you ever been in a place where you are the apple of someone's eye; only to realize that your so-called mate couldn't be farther from the person they portrayed themselves to be?

It's okay. It just wasn't meant to be.

Feel

When you met me, you told me I was gorgeous
Your words never ceased to cover me with
Compliments, loving epithets
A declaration of being your God-sent
Unlike anyone you've ever met
Your gift
My gift
An outlet
Of how you really feel . . .
Or shall I say, felt
Just months ago, I was pretty
Your gaze never ceased to shower me with loving, genuine vitality
A supposed exclamation of punctuality
Your gift
My gift
An outlet
Of how you really feel . . .
Or shall I say, felt
Just weeks ago, I was just cute
You began to tell me you knew I'd wear black
When before you adored me whether or not I had worn the
same outfit back to back
I knew your adoration for me was no longer a fact
But a relinquished release . . .
An outlet
Of how you really feel . . .
Or shall I say, felt
Just days ago, you just looked at me
Cold, bland, no feeling
An unrequited vexation, transfixed upon your face
Now a stranger to me
A total transformation
Of who you used to be . . .

My rock, my soul
My reality
That walked right out of my dreams
Only to be unreal, unrecognizable, lacking zeal . . .
An outlet
Of how you really felt
Or shall I now say,
feel

Snapshot:

My thoughts become treble clefs, half-notes as my soul sings songs of you.

~Kathy M. Walters

ove is a beautifully crafted gift from God. Love is universal. Love is awesome when it is requited and renewed each day.

One of the most beautiful gifts from God is the love shared on a wedding day between the bride and groom.

A Kind of Love

I love you in every way
A glimpse, a smile, a glance
Just the thought of your touch
Illuminates my day
You see, your presence fulfills my every need
You're my H_2O, CO_2, even the oxygen that I breathe
My love grows deeper and deeper over time
Got the love Jones so bad
I had to flow this rhyme
Constantly thanking God
For a man so divine
Heart thumping, soul stirring
About to lose my mind
Going about my day thinking only of you
My thoughts become treble clefs, half-notes
As my soul sings songs of you
Soft whispers, caresses gentle
My vibe is so in sync with you
Ending never
Intertwined forever
Holding hands as we both say, "I do"

snapshot:

Embrace your legacy and love
will find its way.

~ Kathy M. Walters

amily can be defined in so many ways. No matter what your definition may be, embrace it and hold on as tight as you can. Learn to love the ones who may not even appear to love you. Try to make peace during the volatile times and never take on the role of "judge." Believe me; God has that under control all by Himself.

Move away from the shadows of the past and place everything in God's hands. Love Him, love yourself, love life and love your family!

A Continuing Legacy

A continuing legacy
For you, for me
Like a flower needs water
A family needs love, you see
Sure, we've all made mistakes
Along life's way
We've experienced the loss of loved ones
But they're in our hearts each and every day
God places no more on us
Than we can bear
But as a family, we should always love and always be there
Being there for one another
Along life's way
Embracing one another
If any one of us goes astray . . .
A continuing legacy
For you, for me
Like a flower needs water
A family needs that love, you see
For love is the focus
Love is the key
Love is that gift from God
But most of all, love is free
Expressing love doesn't cost a dime
Let our hearts be the focus
For God is our guide
Through strength, courage, togetherness
And faith
We continue our legacy
We embrace our faith
We are a family that stands tall
We're pressing for the mark, for the prize
For the highest call

The family that prays together
Will always stay together
A continuing legacy
For one, for all
A continuing legacy

For you, for me
I love you all
Let us love unconditionally!

snapshot:

> Your account is no longer "spiritually insufficient," and your soul is no longer facing "imminent foreclosure."
>
> ~ Kathy M. Walters

lose your eyes. Imagine there was a holy-ghost filled, fire-baptized Bank of Jesus Christ. Would you take all of your tears, fears, lost hopes and requests to God? If so, you would quickly find that after being in the presence of God, He provides an abundance of blessings, grace and mercy. All you need to do is be obedient, complete your deposit, and allow yourself to be led by faith.

Where to Go

Evolved from the
immaculate formation of a
Deoxyribonucleic acid, also known as
D-N-A
Charismatically crafted and created
by our Omnipotent, Omnipresent, Almighty Creator, God
Reflective of a 360° band of circulation
Symbolizing
A circumference of a love that has no beginning, no middle and no
end.
Authenticated,
never duplicated;
originality in its purest form
We are children of God
But what if?
What if you suddenly awakened and all hope was gone?
What if every blessing God had ever granted you was now a curse?
What if you found that
some of your closest alliances had now turned their backs on you?
What if every stronghold God had delivered you from had gained
momentum and was once again
before you?
Where do you go
when past hurt has moved in,
packed your bags
and is forcing you out
of your own home?
Where do you go?
You go
to the Holy-ghost filled, fire baptized BANK of Jesus Christ
Anxiously anticipating your arrival will be an Angel by the name of
Faith

Faith will ask you a series of questions and send you through tumul-
tuous procedures . . .
Without question, you comply
She then asks you to complete a Slip of Deposit
Now, on that Slip of Deposit, you are to list
every tear,
every fear,
every lost hope
and every request to God
Again, you comply
You sign it, date it and hand it back to Faith
She smiles
She then tells you to wait in the Waiting Area because The President
and CEO is requesting your presence
Again, you comply
So you wait,
and wait . . . . . and wait
Finally, two Angels appear . . .
A set of twins by the names of Grace and Mercy
They each grab a hand and lead you to a huge room where the table
is spread
They place you in a seat
and relax your feet
upon a wooden box
Immediately, you recognize the Man at the head of the table
He is none other than Jesus Christ . . .
The Alpha and Omega,
the beginning and the end,
The same God today that He was yesterday,
the Man who walked on water,
who raised Lazarus from the dead,
who healed Bartameus of blindness,
who fed 5,000 with five loaves and 2 fish,
who calmed the Stormy seas . . .
and there is silence.
It is at this point in time when you realize that
everything you handed to Faith
is now in Jesus' hands

One by one, he begins to stamp each item:
For every tear, FAVOR
For every fear, FAVOR
For every lost hope, FAVOR
Jesus tells you that He is aware of your struggles
And everything you had to go through
He's also aware of just how long you had to wait . . .
And because of your obedience
And your solidarity with Faith
That it was He who allowed Grace and Mercy to see you through
Your account
is no longer "spiritually insufficient"
and your soul is no longer facing
"imminent foreclosure!"
Oh, and by the way . . .
the wooden box where you rested your feet . . .
that is your footstool and your enemies are underneath
So whenever you feel that hope is gone
And you just can't find your way
Seek ye first the kingdom of God
And expect a brighter day
For every struggle,
God gives you double for your trouble . . .
Excuse me, but I have to get to the bank!

Snapshot:

> Always strive for "completion", because perfection does not exist.
>
> ~Kathy M. Walters

Only God has the ability to validate each and every one of us. Sometimes we may feel unloved and unwanted. Our paths in life flow from happy to sad. The most important thing for us to realize is that no one is perfect. We all have flaws, and it isn't over until God says it's over! You can succeed!

Unfit, Unloved: Are You Cast Aside?

You give a smile
You get
A stare
You join the crowd
But, they leave you there
Standing alone,
you wonder, why?
Unfit. Unloved.
Are you cast
aside?
You make an effort
You get put down
That spiraling descension,
level to the ground.
Prevailing questions,
You have to ask
Why are simplicities
your hardest task?
Why are you picked out
to be picked on?
Unfit. Unloved.
A lifetime woven in thorns.
Amazed at how cruel this world can be
Exasperated by bondage,
Just waiting to be free
You don't ask for pity,
but you pray for peace.
You strive for completion,
because perfection doesn't exist, you see.
Speak life to your own discourse
And follow your dreams.
Simply stated, persistently reiterated,
No one validates you but God.

Never, ever spend
God's gift-given time
in negativity.
Your set-back is God's set-up
To merely set you free!
Free from the toils
Served on the platter of life . . .
You were always fit
You were created by God . . .
And you will never be
cast aside.

Snapshot:

"Speak" is a small word with a powerful position.

~Kathy M. Walters

As the saying goes, there is power in the tongue. If you speak positively, you project positive energy. If you speak negatively, you are automatically setting yourself up for failure and disdain. Why would you set yourself up for failure when you hold the power to be the best you can be?

Speak

Out of all the words in the English language
I choose the word, Speak
A small word
With a powerful position
Surpassing the sometimes simplistic definition, Speak
Normally, it is defined as an utter, a salutation
Comparing it to language, oration and articulation
A small word
With a powerful position
Webster should take note
While I articulate my definition
Speak
Is a method by which you
Create diversion
You speak as a weapon
To those who cast aspersions
Speak
Is an antidote
To a poisoned mind
So speak
To mediocrity
Negativity
And lost time
Speak
To those who have hurt you
The friends that deserted you
The ones that second—guessed you
The ones that never heard you
Oh, I don't mean speak
As in an utterance or salutation
I mean speak
Speak to that lifeless situation

Allow the atmosphere to engulf your words so that they
never return void
Make sanity your sanctity
So that peace is now your reward
Out of all the words in the English language
I choose the word speak
A small word with a powerful position
Surpassing the sometimes simplistic definition
Speak
Speak life to those psychologically cataclysmic "isms"
Racism, criticism, antagonism, mental recidivism
A pattern of thinking the same
Being mentally enslaved
So messed up in the mind
You don't know from whence you came
Just Speak
From one generation to another
That generational curse
Speak to that methodical crutch
You've obviously carried since birth
Speak life to all the nay—sayers
At home, at work and at church
Just speak into the atmosphere
It's all about doing God's work
See, I'm just a vessel in this master plan
My weapon of speak will definitely withstand
Try to taint my integrity, my joy at hand
I will only speak it into existence again
Out of all the words in the English language,
I choose the word, Speak
A small word with a powerful position
Surpassing the sometimes simplistic definition
Speak

Snapshot:

A brighter day . . . always hoped for, slowly progressing . . . but definitely on its way.

~Kathy M. Walters

Has it ever seemed that everything that could possibly go wrong has gone wrong? Have you ever gone into your secret closet and begun to ask God some deep questions? Have you ever been that bold Christian and had the audacity to ask God, "Why?"

God knows our heart. Deep down, we know that God's word will not return void. After you have made your requests known, your plea heard . . . sit back and watch what God can do. Your breakthrough is definitely on the way!

Breakthrough

Have you ever been
In that peculiar place
Where the spotlight
Was on you?
Not for fame
Not for fortune
But simply because of what you were
Going through . . .
Through those tests
And trials in life
Like a ship
Being tossed at sea
You've asked the question
Over and over
"Lord, Lord, why me?
I've pressed for the mark
I've kept the faith
I've prayed both night and day
But yet
I'm still standing
Right here
Saddened and filled with dismay . . .
I've called your name
So many times
Seems no answer, no sign, no reply
All I hear is the sound of my own voice
Circling back to me
With a resounding, "Why?"
I am Your child
This is Your word
So, I'm standing boldly before the throne of grace
Lord, ease my pain
Order my steps

Put my trials in a place
That's far away
That ceases to exist
So I claim this
In your son Jesus' name
I'm worn from fighting
I'm weary from crying
My faith cannot be in vain!
All I need is a word from You, Lord
In You, I will always abide
And so,
Make me
Mold me
Strengthen me
Console me
Lord, please don't leave my side
Comfort me
In this time
Of my storm
Be my wheel in the middle of a wheel
Lead me to that rock
That is higher than I
Let me hear you say,
"Peace, be still"
For my world is filled
With so much turmoil these days
Seems as though hope is sometimes gone
I can't help but wonder
Why sometimes doing right seems wrong
It takes all I have just to hold on
Questions, problems
Convoluting my mind
Decisions, lost visions
Feels like I'm running out of time
Destruction, obstruction
Can't see my way through . . .
Now grace and mercy . . .
Where are you?

Wait, wait
I hear a voice
And yes, it's crystal clear
He's letting me know
He's still in control
Always has been and always will
So listen
While God speaks:
Child, child
What is wrong with you?
Have you forgotten everything you've ever learned?
I heard you
When you called me
I watched you
When you doubted me
All you needed was time
Time to just wait
While I do
What I do
Help was definitely on its way
Let patience have its perfect work
Be anxious for nothing, I say
When you thought I had left you
It was then that I was oh so near
I wiped your eyes
As you wept at night
You didn't even notice me there
I held you
In your darkest hours
I gently squeezed your hands
I'm always ordering your steps, you see
Leading you to the ultimate plan
You see, you had to cry
You were commissioned to fight
But it was only to make you strong
I had to break you
Before I could transform, mend and make you
For hope was never gone

I am the great I Am
Fear not, for this is true
Peace, be still . . .
Now, dry those tears
And rejoice,
It's time for your breakthrough!

PART 6

Pillars of Positivity

There are four regions: North, South, East and West.

There are four seasons: Winter, Spring, Summer and Fall.

There are four segments of the day: Dawn, Noon,
Evening, and Night.

There are four elements: Earth, Air, Fire and Water.

Thus, the Four Pillars of Positivity reflects:

The region of Grace
The season to Forgive
The segment of Faith
The element of Mercy

GRACE

God's

Redemption

And

Covering for

Everyone

FORGIVE

Finding

Order

Restoration and

Grace

In

Virtually

Everything

FAITH

Finally

Accomplishing the

Impossible

Through

Him

MERCY

May

Emmanuel's

Righteousness

Cover

You

PART 7

Positive Perspectives

Positive Perspectives

Trust in the Lord with all thine heart; and lean not to thine own understanding.

Proverbs 3:5

Ask, and it shall be given you; seek, and ye shall find; knock, and it shall be opened unto you.

Matthew 7:7

Take therefore no thought for the morrow; for the morrow shall take thought for the things of itself. Sufficient unto the day is the evil thereof.

Matthew 6:34

But they that wait upon the Lord shall renew their strength; they shall mount up as eagles; they shall run, and not be weary; and they shall walk, and not faint.

Isaiah 40:31

And the peace of God, which passeth all understanding, shall keep your hearts and minds through Christ Jesus.

Philippians 4:7

PART 8

Pills for Your Pain
Promise for Your Prayers
Power for Your Praise
The Word and the Melody

Pills for Your Pain

(The Word)

Rejoiceth not in iniquity, but rejoiceth in the truth. Beareth all things, believeth all things, hopeth all things, endureth all things.

1 Corinthians 13:6-7

For I know the thoughts that I think toward you, saith the Lord, thoughts of peace, and not of evil, to give you an expected end. Then shall ye call upon me, and ye shall go and pray unto me, and I will hearken unto you. And ye shall seek me, when ye shall search for me with all your heart.

Jeremiah 29: 11-13

The Lord also will be a refuge for the oppressed, a refuge in times of trouble. And they that know thy name will put their trust in thee: for thou, Lord, has not forsaken them that seek thee.

Psalm 9: 9-10

Above all taking the shield of faith, wherewith ye shall be able to quench all the fiery darts of the wicked. And take the helmet of salvation, and the sword of the Spirit, which is the word of God.

Ephesians 6: 16-17

And not only so, but we glory in tribulations also: knowing that tribulation worketh patience; And patience, experience; and experience hope. And hope maketh not ashamed; because the love of God is shed abroad in our hearts by the
Holy Ghost which is given unto us.

Romans 5: 3-5

Pills for Your Pain

(The Melody)

Father Can You Hear Me
Artist: Tamela Mann

I Feel a Breakthrough
Artist: Norman Hutchins

Hold On
Artist: James Fortune and Fiya
(Featuring Monica and Fred Hammond)

Promise for Your Prayers

(The Word)

Confess your faults one to another, and pray one for another,
that ye may be healed. The effectual fervent prayer of a
righteous man availeth much.

James 5:16

And all things, whatsoever ye shall ask in prayer,
believing, ye shall receive.

Matthew 21:22

If my people, which are called by my name, shall humble them-
selves, and pray, and seek my face, and turn from their wicked ways;
then will I hear from heaven, and will forgive their sin,
and will heal their land.

2 Chronicles 7:14

Pray without ceasing.

1Thessalonians 5:17

Evening, and morning, and at noon, will I pray,
and cry aloud: and he shall hear my voice.

Psalm 55:17

Promise for Your Prayers

(The Melody)

Nobody Greater
Artist: VaShawn Mitchell

The Prayer
Artist: Yolanda Adams and Donnie McClurkin

Let the Church Say Amen
Artist: Andrae Crouch and Marvin Winans

Power for Your Praise

(The Word)

Because thy lovingkindness is better than life, my lips shall praise thee. Thus will I bless thee while I live: I will lift up my hands in thy name. My soul shall be satisfied with marrow and fatness; and my mouth shall praise thee with joyful lips.

Psalm 63: 3-5

One generation shall praise thy works to another, and shall declare thy mighty acts.

Psalm 145:4

All thy works shall praise thee, O Lord; and thy saints shall bless thee.

Psalm 145:10

Praise ye the Lord. Praise ye the Lord from the heavens:
praise him in the heights.

Psalm 148:1

Let them praise the name of the Lord; for he commanded,
and they were created.

Psalm 148:5

Power for Your Praise

(The Melody)

Praise Is What I Do
Artist: William Murphy

In the Middle
Artist: Isaac Carree

Holy Ghost Power
Artist: The Chicago Mass Choir

PART 9

Pensive Pause:

- Giving Back (Sharing your Spiritual Gifts)
  - Determine Your Goals
  - Taking Care of You
(What do you want out of life?)
  - Create a Plan of Action

Giving Back

Sharing your Spiritual Gifts

1 Cor 12:1-12* Romans 12:8-10* Ephesians 4:11

Are you aware that everyone has a spiritual gift? Spiritual gifts are natural and can also be labeled as "miraculous." Spiritual gifts are granted by the Holy Spirit.

Though gifts are beheld by individuals, collectively they function for the benefit of others and for the benefit of the church as a whole. Spiritual gifts include; but are not limited to: teaching, healing, interpretations of tongues, leadership, giving, prophesy serving, exhortation and mercy.

Discover your gift and give back! Share what the Holy Spirit has given for the good of God's kingdom.

Determine Your Goals

*I*n order to achieve anything, you must see it and believe it. Concentrate on the positive. Focus on creating the positive future you so rightfully deserve!

And the Lord answered me, and said, Write the vision, and make it plain upon tables, that he may run that readeth it.

For the vision is yet for an appointed time, but at the end it shall speak, and not lie: though it tarry, wait for it; because it will surely come and not tarry.

Habakkuk 2:2-3

Taking Care of You

What do you want out of life?

- What makes you smile?
- What makes you laugh?
- What are some of the things you would do for free because you enjoy them so much?
- What makes you feel special?
- What makes you feel as though you are fulfilling your purpose in life?
- What do you really want to do in life?
- What would you like to be doing in the next six months?
- What are your dreams?

Create a Plan of Action to Execute Your Goal(s)

- Define your goal.
- Determine how it will make a difference in your life.
- State the purpose of your goal.
- Decide which steps are needed in order to achieve this goal.
- Determine how much research, if any, is needed.
- Decide whether or not you will need to consult with someone or team with a mentor.
- Set a target date to begin.

Go for it!

PART 10

Path to Progression

Insurance

PPIP

There are several things we are required to have in life if our desire is to be protected. There are many things in life we need to acquire in order to feel more secure.

If you want to drive, you must have a driver's license. If you want to protect yourself, others and your vehicle, you will need automobile insurance.

In the event you are hospitalized or need medical maintenance or medical attention, you will need health insurance.

Let's take this a step further. I want to provide you with the **Pain to Praise Insurance Plan.**

Included in this plan:

- Prayer
- Pain to Praise Credo: *Essential Beliefs of the Christian Faith*
- Seven Steps: The Cycle of Completion
- Notice of Eviction
- Life Application Checklist
- Relax, Release, Rebuild, Renew
- Pulling It All Together
- God Said It And That Settles It!

Prayer

Lord, I thank you for this day. I thank you for who you are and for the magnitude with which you created all things. I thank you for Your Son, for Your Word, and for the Holy Spirit. I ask that I might place my faith entirely in you so that you may increase within me. I ask you to forgive me for my sins and to create in me the spirit of forgiveness toward others.

I ask you to bless those who are sick physically and spiritually wounded by their transgressions and in dire need of your presence.

I ask you to remove anything from me that is hindering my peace of mind. Lord, please loosen any strongholds or infirmities which belie my body, spirit or soul. Create in me a clean heart and the burning desire to do your will, and to abandon my own will.

These and many more blessings I ask, in your precious, powerful and matchless name. In Jesus' name I pray.

Amen

Pain to Praise Credo:

Essential Beliefs of the Christian Faith

If we confess our sins and believe Jesus was resurrected, we shall experience the joy of salvation.

That if thou shalt confess with thy mouth the Lord Jesus, and shalt believe in thine heart that God hath raised him from the dead, thou shalt be saved. For with the heart man believeth unto righteousness; and with the mouth confession is made unto salvation. (Romans 10: 9-10)

Jesus is love.

For God so loved the world, that he gave his only begotten Son, that whosoever believeth in him should not perish, but have everlasting life. (John 3:16)

God is the creator of all things.

In the beginning God created the heaven and the earth. (Genesis 1:1)

God is three in one (Father, Son, and Holy Spirit/Trinity).

Elect according to the foreknowledge of God the Father, through sanctification of the Spirit, unto obedience and sprinkling of the blood of Jesus Christ: Grace unto you, and peace, be multiplied. (1 Peter 1:2)

God is omnipotent (all powerful).

And I heard as it were the voice of a great multitude, and as the voice of many waters, and as the voice of mighty thunderings, saying, Alleluia: for the Lord God omnipotent reigneth. (Revelation 19:6)

God is omniscient (knows all things).

For if our heart condemn us, God is greater than our heart, and knoweth all things. (1 John 3:20)

There is only one God.

Ye are my witnesses, saith the Lord, and my servant whom I have chosen: that ye may know and believe me, and understand that I am he: before me there was no God formed, neither shall there be after me. (Isaiah 43:14)

God is omnipresent (present everywhere).

Am I a God at hand, saith the Lord, and not a God afar off?

Can any hide himself in secret places that I shall not see him? saith the Lord. Do not I fill heaven and earth? saith the Lord. (Jeremiah 23:23, 24)

Jesus was born to the virgin, Mary.

And the angel said unto her, Fear not, Mary: for thou hast found favour with God.

And behold, thou shalt conceive in thy womb, and bring forth a son, and shalt call his name Jesus.

(Luke 1:30-31)

Seven Steps:

The Cycle of Completion

Step 1: Confess your sins to God.
Step 2: Acknowledge the stronghold(s) in your life.
Step 3: Communicate how it (they) make you feel.
Step 4: Ask God to loose the enemy's stronghold(s) in your life.
Step 5: Place the precious blood of Jesus over your life's situation.
Step 6: Trust in God, believe in His word, turn everything over to him.
Step 7: Release the negative and let it go!

List any strongholds you wish to overcome.

1. _____
2. _____
3. _____
4. _____
5. _____
6. _____
7. _____

IMPORTANT

In order to help you become free of strongholds, please complete the next section as a symbolic agreement to re-claim everything that rightfully belongs to you.

<u>Notice:</u>

Notice of Eviction

Name of Tenant (List everything that applies)**:**

_____
_____
_____
_____
_____ .

Date to terminate tenancy: **<u>Immediately</u>**

Please Take Notice that pursuant to the agreement I have with <u>My Lord and Savior, Jesus Christ,</u> you are hereby ordered to vacate the premise of my joy right now.

Please Take Further Notice that you are <u>immediately</u> commanded to return everything you took from my place of peace.
Failure to adhere to this notice will result in repercussions from a power far greater than I. Consider yourself warned . . .

Signed,

_____

Life Application Checklist

~

- ☐ Always put God first
- ☐ Decide what is important to you
- ☐ Rid yourself of pride
- ☐ Prioritize
- ☐ Release fear
- ☐ Take care of others, but don't lose focus of self. Be sure to take care of you.
- ☐ Determine what is least important to you
- ☐ Allow no one to steal your joy
- ☐ Forgive
- ☐ Love
- ☐ Learn from your mistakes
- ☐ Ask God for the Spirit of Discernment
- ☐ Remain positive
- ☐ Realize that you can't please everyone
- ☐ Stay prayerful
- ☐ Smile
- ☐ Be humble
- ☐ Be grateful
- ☐ Know that it is okay to cry sometimes
- ☐ Realize that it is okay to ask for help sometimes
- ☐ Accept the fact that it is okay to say "no" sometimes
- ☐ Never place man on a pedestal. He is subject to failure.
- ☐ Don't be hard on yourself
- ☐ Believe in yourself, but believe in God more
- ☐ Go against the grain sometimes
- ☐ Exercise your faith
- ☐ Realize that when all else fails, just wait on the Lord. He will always pull you through!

Relax* Release* Rebuild* Renew

Relax. Find a quiet place to sit or lie down. Make yourself comfortable. Take slow, deep breaths.
Note: If you like, play soft jazz or purchase a CD featuring nature's sounds if you don't already have one.

Release. Release negative energy by making the decision to forgive and forego holding grudges or holding onto pains of the past.

Rebuild. Start over. Walk away from the old and begin re-building your life on a solid foundation.

Renew. Embrace change and become excited about starting fresh, starting over. Begin living life to its fullest potential!

Pulling It All Together

People may ask you why or how you can smile in the midst of what you're going through, or better yet, what you've been through. They weren't there to witness your "darkness before the dawn" or your "midnight hour." They may not have known that your midnight lasted all day long. They have no idea how many times you've had to command your storm to move away and stay out of your life. But you know what? We all have a story to tell.

One viable option is to place the precious blood of Jesus over every tear, every mountain and every negative aspect within the most miniscule distance of your goals and dreams. Negativity plays no role in your success. It has no place within your family, your relationships, your home, your job, your life or your spirit.

Through faith and restoration, you can conquer anything. You must let go of everything that previously held you captive. No longer accept the position or label of being spiritually, mentally or unfavorably bound.

Set yourself free from everything that hindered you from the blessings you so rightfully deserve!

Praise Him!

God Said It and That Settles It!

Where there is no vision, the people perish: but he that keepeth the law, happy is he.

Proverbs 29:18

A Reading Group Guide

From Pain to Praise
Kathy M. Walters

ABOUT THIS GUIDE

This guide is designed to facilitate conversation
within reading groups.

Questions for Discussion

1) How did you feel about the Open Letter? Could you relate to the poetry?

2) Which poem seemed to be speaking directly to you?

3) Did the poems or words of inspiration help you deal with any particular situation or challenge you are currently going through?

4) Were you inspired by God's Lemonade?

5) Is there a topic you would have liked to be addressed that was not included in this book?

6) Discuss your favorite poem.

7) Is there a poem or words of inspiration that you would recommend to someone else?

8) How did you feel about the Haiku section?

9) Following this section is a sneak preview of Kathy M. Walters' upcoming novella, My Cup Runneth Over. Did you enjoy the sneak preview?

10) Did you like the idea of a sneak preview?

11) Kathy M. Walters wanted to write a book illustrating the transparency and fluctuation between imperfection, pain and praise. Did you get a feel of this while reading this book? If so, how did you feel about this?

Turn the page for a sneak preview of
Kathy M. Walters' upcoming novella,

MY CUP RUNNETH OVER

As I look over my life,
I see time:
I cherish it
I envy it
I embrace it
I regret it
It has made me laugh
It has made me shed tears
It has blessed me one hundred fold
It has weakened my soul
It has given me friends
It has taken them
It has enabled me to see
It has blinded me
It has comforted me
It has deceived me
It used to bind me
But now, I am set free
I see my future
I know God
He covers me

He knows my heart
He keeps me
He makes me
He molds me
He validates me
He always leads me
He always cares
He's everything
He's everywhere
He's joy
He's abundance
He constantly makes me grow
He places my cup before me
He pours . . . He pours . . .
He pours . . .
And it overflows!

My Cup Runneth Over
~Kathy M. Walters

Prologue

"**I** now baptize you in the name of the Father, in the name of the Son and in the name of the Holy Ghost." I think back on that day and I can recall every detail as if it happened just yesterday. A few weeks prior to that special Sunday, I stood before the pastor and the entire congregation professing my belief in Jesus Christ, acknowledging that Jesus is the Son of God and believing that Jesus died for my sins.

My family and I had been attending services for a couple of months when we unanimously decided that First Trinity Baptist was the place to be. Even the church's name seemed synonymous to a description of esteem and grandeur. The mere thought of the word trinity as being part of the name in our place of worship assured us that if we joined this church, we couldn't go wrong. Actually, I had no idea what trinity meant at the time, but after I observed the manner in which others reacted and loved the name, it sounded good to me, too. So, I would go around telling everyone I knew that I was attending the best church in town . . . First Trinity Baptist.

First Trinity Baptist was like a home away from home. It was located about twenty minutes from where we lived and I can still remember how excited I would become on Saturday nights as I contemplated what to wear for Sunday service. Every day in our household was special, but Sunday seemed to be the core of quality time and what family was all about.

Each Sunday morning, my siblings and I would awaken to the sound of gospel music playing on the radio, the laughter and familiar chatter of my parents in the kitchen, the wonderful aroma of Maxwell House coffee and the mouthwatering smell of bacon, eggs, cheese grits and buttered toast. We would all sit around the table, bless the food and reflect on the previous week and the week ahead. My parents constantly stressed the importance of striving for excellence and were always telling us to "be prepared for the spills of life". With a puzzled look on my face, I would think, *What does that mean?* and *Why are they always saying that?* I refused to ask for yet another explanation. I have asked countless times. In answering, one of them would simply say, "One day you will understand. You have to go through some things in order to see some things." I digress.

My younger brother, Austin and I were required to keep a journal. In the journal we would record our goals, accomplishments and any challenges we faced during the week. My baby sister, Carmen was only 2 years old, so her only goal in life was to determine where and when she would throw another one of her famous temper tantrums.

Austin and I were both dreamers. We had a lot of similarities, but we also had a lot of differences. Austin, 8 was always talking about how he wanted to travel the world and preach the Gospel. I was amazed at how Austin would grab his Bible, stand behind the television stand as his podium and "play church". Carmen and I would sit on the sofa, which Austin insisted we refer to as "pews" and listen to his sermon. I believe Austin had watched so many crusades and studied the mannerisms and context of so many ministers that he was actually good at it. He always had a prepared a scripture, a text, a message and bullet-points on how to apply the message to everyday life. Sometimes my parents would come in and sit quietly as the sermon was taking place. The strange thing is that we all felt great afterwards and we always walked away with some powerful food for thought.

At the tender age of ten, I knew my destiny was to write books, poetry and connect with people and their problems on a more intimate level. My ultimate goal was to become a psychiatrist. I wanted to know how and why people behaved the way they do. I was overly inquisitive and intrigued with the mind. I knew that if given the chance, I could reach people by tapping into the core of their souls and making a positive impact. Sometimes, I would daydream and drift away into another world just thinking about how I could make a difference.

So after breakfast was over, Austin insisted that he lead us in prayer before walking out of the door. As usual, I had to get one last sip of water and run to my room to grab my purse. Excited and anxious, we were on our way!

First Trinity Baptist was known for its "soul-stirring" pastor, breathtakingly-beautiful landscape and for its loving, friendly congregation. Every time we approached the church; I would always admire its beauty and feel an overwhelming sense of serenity.

Upon arrival at the church gate, there was a simple white sign with royal blue lettering that read: First Trinity Baptist Church. Where our motto is: God First. As we proceed down the long, winding driveway, there were huge magnolia trees on either side. Along the way, there were other signs that read: "Welcome", "Jesus Loves You" and "Thanks for sharing with us". As if the scenery along the pathway to the church wasn't mesmerizing enough, as soon as you turn the final corner, out of nowhere appeared a cascade of tulips, hyacinth, daffodils and autumn crocus. The entire arrangement was formed into the capital letter, T, and encircled by heart-shaped hedges.

Parking was never a problem. There were always several gentlemen in dark blue suits directing each car to an appointed parking space.

Each gentleman had a huge smile on his face and I can assure you that this was just the beginning of the welcome fest. I was so impressed the first time it rained because before we had a chance to exit the car, we were greeted by two gentlemen with huge, blue umbrellas and they escorted us directly into the church. Once inside the vestibule, a member from the Hospitality Committee greeted us with more smiles and offered us a church program.

I couldn't wait to be seated so that I could hear the choir sing. After the Devotion, Morning Hymn and the Welcome, it was finally time for my favorite part of service. Austin, Carmen and I were well versed on the importance of church and how we were to behave once inside. But needless to say, we were still children. We sat attentively and observed everything that took place. But as the pastor approached the pulpit, adorned in his black robe, carrying his huge Bible and chained eyeglasses, my siblings and I would glance at each other in great anticipation. We had one common thought, "It's show time!"

Although I had attended church for as long as I could remember, that "shouting" thing still got me every time! I knew better! But, Sunday after Sunday, my parents would have to scold my siblings and me for laughing at some point in time. We would giggle so hard that we would become weak and fall over on each other like a line of dominoes. Carmen would always get crushed because somehow she always managed to be sitting at the end of the pew by the time the pastor was about to deliver his sermon. Children's Church was not an option for Carmen because my parents knew that at any given moment she would be escorted right back into the main sanctuary. Carmen had a way of misbehaving in Children's Church, but she behaved as the lesser of two evils as long as she was seated with the family.

One particular Sunday, after Reverend Freemont preached his sermon, he stepped down from the pulpit and began singing "Jesus, You're the Center of My Joy". This was a church favorite and as soon as the music began to play, people stood up and began praising the Lord. In seconds, nearly half of the choir members had fallen over the pews, the pianist fell backwards onto the steps and we saw three shoes flying mid-air! One of the ushers ended up head-butting a woman that she was trying to console when the Holy Ghost got a hold of her too! The woman's hat and wig fell onto the floor and so did both the usher and the now hatless woman! On any other Sunday, this would have been a book of classic moments. But for some reason, there was no laughter today. A sense of calm overshadowed me. I can't explain it. I've never felt that way before. But I enjoyed whatever was happening to me. I look back today and realize that obviously my experience was nothing short of worship, witnessing and being surrounded by the presence of God. Pastor Freedmont finished the song and was now opening the doors of the church. In an instant, I stood up and looked directly at my family. One by one, our eyes met and it was as if we communicated without saying a word. I lead as my entire family walked down the aisle, surrounding me. Austin grabbed my hand. We both gave our lives to Christ. The entire congregation was in an uproar and cried tears of joy as people were coming from everywhere to begin a brand new life. I looked around and witnessed people coming down from the balcony, the side aisles and from the back of the church. From each moment thereafter, there was a trail of touching events taking place. Just when we thought there was a final count of those who were giving their lives to Christ, another family came down.

There was a very tall, somewhat muscular, middle-aged man that cried uncontrollably as he approached the pastor along with his wife and children. He introduced himself as Raymond White. Mr. White asked for forgiveness as he promised God and the entire church family that he would never lay a hand on his wife or children again.

The pastor then prayed for a young mother holding the tiny hand of her two and a half year old daughter. The young mother whispered something to the pastor and he calmly embraced her and whispered into her ear. The mother whispered in Pastor Freemont's ear and the two of them went back and forth for what seemed like an eternity. Finally, Pastor Freemont just threw his head back and looked up to the sky as tears rolled down his face. When the young mother, now identified as Rowan Gilbert, gave her testimony, she said she wanted everyone to know that three weeks ago, she stood in the doctor's office and wept as the doctor told her that her precious daughter had been diagnosed with a pituitary tumor.

Well, she went on to explain how she prayed and asked God to heal her daughter. Rowan Gilbert stated that on yesterday, she took her daughter back into the office for a follow-up visit and the tumor could not be found. The MRI was clear.

The entire church was on their feet crying, shouting, praying and once again thanking God. After the traditional questions and being formally welcomed by the pastor, the church secretary asked everyone who had come down to follow her into the conference room where she and two short, gray-haired women told us what to expect and what events would take place from this point. Austin and I were told that we would be baptized on November 7 at the 11:00 am service. We were also instructed to arrive an hour early on the day of baptism, wearing both white underwear and white socks. We were told we would be provided with white robes and towels. This was so awesome. I couldn't wait.

On the day of the baptism, I was both excited and nervous. My excitement derived from the entire concept of who God is and what good things were in store for me. I was nervous because I was afraid of water. A couple of years before, I had nearly drowned at the neighborhood park when my dad took me to swimming lessons. Everyone but me knew how to swim, so the new swimming instructor, Mr. Marks, convinced me that he could help me conquer my fear and teach me how to swim. I will never forget that day. For some dreadful reason, Mr. Marks was under the delusional assumption that his "method" of forcing my head under water would turn me into an Olympic swimmer and cure my fear. Are you kidding me?

Once I went under and the water covered my entire body, I saw my entire life flash before my eyes. I could see everything I had ever done. I saw the good times, the bad times, and things I thought I had forgotten all about. I'd heard people talk about seeing their life flash before their eyes, but I am here to tell you that it was like nothing I have ever experienced. After the water filled my lungs, I passed out. I can remember finally coughing and feeling a burning sensation in my eyes, ears, throat and chest. I was exhausted, cold and shaking. It was awful.

As I squinted my eyes into focus, I saw two firemen kneeling over me and a crowd of people in the background. Thank God there was a fire station directly across the street. I later realized that I had almost lost my life. I had to be resuscitated by those two firemen. With all the commotion and chaos, it wasn't until I had gotten myself together that I realized that my bathing suit top was missing. I could only think that not only was I half-dead, but I was also half-dressed!

Two women immediately came over and draped a towel around me. I wept silently and promised myself that I would never go near water again. Since that traumatizing experience even up to now, I have been terrified of water.

So, when it was my turn to be baptized, I began having a panic attack. I prayed, "Lord, I'm just a child. Don't take me yet. I nearly drowned a few years ago and you saved me . . ." In a split second, the next thing I knew . . . .

"I now baptize you in the name of the Father, in the name of the Son and in the name of the Holy Ghost". I was dipped so quickly that once under water it felt as if everything was moving in slow motion. While underneath, I could hear the muffled sounds of the organ and voices all around me. I could also hear and feel my heart racing at an all-time high. Once again, I was fighting a panic attack. *Help me, God. Please help me!* I couldn't see. I couldn't breathe. After I emerged, I gasped for air and felt relieved that I was still alive. No firemen, no resuscitation. Just God. Suddenly, there was calm. Streams of water were now flowing from the pure white towel that had been draped around my head. I thought, *Wow. It is as if God and all that He has in store for me is raining down on me.* As I reflect on that moment, I realize that this may just explain the calm and serenity I still feel when it rains. I absolutely love the rain.

I remember the drive home and how happy I was. Everything seemed brand new. The trees appeared greener. The sun shone brighter. It was the happiest beginning of the rest of my life. All I could think was, *I have found God and life is great. From this point on, my life and the lives of those surrounding me are going to be perfect!*

Man, was I wrong.

Twenty Two Years Later . . .

Chapter 1

McKinley

I had been on cloud nine since early this morning, when I received a phone call from Mr. Ellis Powell, CEO of Powell and Powell Consulting. PPC is the premiere firm of its kind. It is known for recruiting the nation's top notch psychiatrists and partnering them with some of the most notable research projects in the arena. I met Mr. Powell about six weeks earlier, when I served as one of three keynote speakers at the 14th Annual Conference for Psychiatrists in South Dakota. The topics discussed for this particular day were Methodologies of Research and Mental Health. Mr. Powell and I spoke at length following my presentation, after which he and the entire room recognized me with a three—minute standing ovation. I felt so honored.

Immediately after Mr. Powell introduced himself, he had many questions and seemed genuinely intrigued by my research methods and assessments. He was very pleasant and told me that he would like to have one of my business cards as he would love to contact me in the near future. I have attended many events and I have met the top executives of many organizations. Therefore, I'm used to the "let's do lunch soon" or "give me your card and we'll discuss this further over dinner." So, I handed Mr. Powell one of the new business cards I specifically had printed for this conference, we shook hands and I made my way around the room. I was beaming inside as I smiled and met with the other conferees. My MO was business as usual. I didn't think anything more of my conversation with Mr. Powell. So, I was startled when the phone rang this morning and I read the words *Powell and Powell* and the area code 605 appeared on my caller Id screen.

"Hello?" I nearly dropped the phone upon answering.

"Good morning. This is Ellis Powell. May I speak to Mckinley Thompson, please?"

"Yes. This is Mckinley Thompson. How are you, Mr. Powell?"

"Great. Fantastic. But, I could be a lot better if you could help me out, though. And please, call me Ellis." I thought, *My goodness, he gets straight to the point, and he wants me to call him "Ellis".* His tone was so upbeat and pleasant.

"Well, how may I help you out, Ellis?" I chuckled as I was now feeling a bit more comfortable and at ease, but still wondering what I could possibly do for Ellis Powell.

After all, he was one of the most powerful and influential men in the northwest region. Ellis cleared his throat and continued, "I have a special assignment that has your name written all over it. I was blown away by your presentation at the annual conference. Our firm would be insane not to consider you for this project."

I could almost hear a slight plea in his voice. He was nothing like I had imagined. I mean, when I met Ellis at the conference, he was very nice, but my one—on—one experience with him was nothing like the person many had described. From all accounts, Ellis Powell had been labeled as a great businessman with no personality. "He's fair, but he's very difficult to work with." "He is hardcore and nothing more". I knew immediately that I needed to get to know Mr. Powell for myself.

That's what's wrong with so many people today. They find a need to listen to what others say and judge people solely by what they have heard, not from what they know or have experienced for themselves. That's a huge injustice. It's also elementary. Some p*eople just need to grow up,* I thought to myself.

"Ms. Thompson?" My thoughts were now interrupted as the voice of someone new chimed in.

"Yes?" I answered after a brief pause. I also realized that I was now on speakerphone.

"Good morning, Ms. Thompson. This is Arlen Winters. I am the Recruiting Manager for PPC. Ellis has been raving about your presentation and has personally selected you for an important research project with J Research Group here in South Dakota."

All I heard were the words, J Research Group. I nearly fainted. This was like a dream come true! Anybody who is somebody in the field of psychiatry has JRG listed on their curriculum vitae. I have been praying for an opportunity like this for what seems like forever. I have no idea what the assignment is, but I am definitely anxious find out.

"Ms. Thompson?" I was still trying to process everything I was hearing.

"Yes. I'm here." I quickly interjected.

"Ms. Thompson, we hope this isn't too short notice, but we would love to meet with you by the end of next week to discuss the specifics of the assignment. We have also spoken to your director, Dr. Williams, and he was honored to approve your leave to work with JRG. Moreover, Powell and Powell will match your base pay for six months in addition to the fee for services provided by JRG. Does this sound like good news for you, Ms. Thompson?

Good news? This is great! If this is any ndication of what is to come, I love it already.

I sighed as I regained my composure. I was smiling from cheek to cheek.

"The pleasure is all mine, Ellis. Thank you, Mr. Winters. I am honored to have this opportunity and I look forward to seeing you both next week."

"Great. I will have my assistant fax over the preliminaries and we will express courier your packet within the hour." Ellis said excitedly.

Ellis and Arlen both bid their good-byes to McKinley and were just about to leave as the door slowly opened in the conference room. They both looked at each other and quickly turned their attention toward the door as the applause began.

Dressed in a classy, designer suit and five—inch Manolo Blahniks strolls in Satan's little sister in the flesh. "Great job, gentlemen!

Bravo for that performance. I was watching and listening via the surveillance camera.

You did just as you were instructed. Little Miss Perfect has taken the bait, hook, line and sinker. Now, you just reel in Ms. McKinley Thompson and make sure she does exactly as she is told. If she doesn't, let's just say that you would find more pleasure sliding down a razor blade into a deep pool of red hot peppers or my name isn't Rowan Gilbert."

Rowan Gilbert was definitely one to be reckoned with. She sashayed toward the door, stopped dead in her tracks, and dramatically spun around, displaying a conniving smirk on her face. "Oh. And Arlen, I will see you at the house tonight." Then she gently closed the door behind her and slowly disappeared.

My Cup Runneth Over

Coming Soon!

Dedications

would like to dedicate this book to several angels who are graciously adorning their wings in heaven. You are still more precious than gold and you have made an indelible mark on my life that can never be duplicated. I miss you, and I think about you always. I will never, ever forget you. I have shed countless tears knowing that you're gone. I have solace in knowing that we will meet again.

Until then . . . I love you. Peace.

My wonderful aunt, Bertha Fowler
My loving uncle, J.D. Walters
My beloved "Mil", Ms. Fern Miller
My dear friend, Racine Foster

Impossible without You

I give thanks to God, for allowing me to realize my dream of becoming an author and inviting others to visit the window of my soul. My backbone, R.L. Walters and Doris Walters, the best parents ever! Jacquelyn and Gary Talley, Courtney, Chaz and Kevin Talley, Regina and Doug Miller, Donovan and David Miller, Randall Walters, Amanda Harper, Rashad, Adrianna, Joshua and Amiyah Walters and John Jones. You have supported me through thick and thin and have always encouraged me to follow my dreams. You mean the world to me and I couldn't have done it without you! Janice Fowler, my beautiful, sweet and loving cousin. Thanks for always making me laugh. I am grateful for your strong, warm, kind and giving spirit. Much love. Fay Alice Walker (Favortwou Publishing) publisher, author, mentor and friend. Thanks a million for showing me the ropes and suggesting that I "just do it."

A.C. Booker-Higgins, Lisa Tyler, you are endlessly supportive and totally awesome! Thanks for being a huge part of my life. There is a reason we share the same birthday! I love you dearly! Myra Surratt-Walters, thank you so much for everything. A lot of what I do has your special touch somewhere in the mix!

Jacqueline Washington (Job Coach Jacqui) thanks for being my friend, mentor, teacher, and motivator. Lots of love. Gwen Jeffcoat, thanks for your friendship, motivation, kindness, warm spirit, and for being so genuine. You have been my rock. Barbara Williams, thank you for your support early on, glad you enjoyed the CD. I appreciate you!

Darlene Lanier and Nancy Smith, thanks for being excited for me and making me feel special. And yes, I heard you clapping for me while I was on stage.

Elaine Tucker, thanks for the laughs, wisdom and kind words. I appreciate it.

LaKeacha Jett, where do I begin? I appreciate you for being my "book buddy." Thanks for the kind words, continuous support, motivation and inspiration and for always having my back. I wish you much success!

Stacy Randle, Anna Williams-Wester and Renita Gibbs, you are three beautiful women inside and out. You are filled with so many gifts. You inspire and encourage me and you definitely "have it going on." Thanks for being there when I needed you most. Much love. Malessia Moses, thanks for always showing interest in my events and what I have planned next. I appreciate you.

Donna Riggins Jones, you have been humble, kind, and inspiring since we were little girls. Monica Lewis Bland, forever a beautiful rose. Thanks! Zoe Daniel, thanks for the beautiful smile and kind words of inspiration. Joyce Clark, you have no idea how your kind words made an impact on me. Thanks!

Christopher Johnson thanks for your friendship, support and kindness.

Tommy Allen thanks for listening, the laughter, and being so supportive of all that I do. I am so grateful. To my look-alike sister and friend, Michelle Brown: thanks for being so kind, gracious and supportive.

I think you're the best. Barbara Williams, thanks for the chats, the smiles and the support. Robert L. Washington, thank you for always encouraging and looking out for me! Angelia Hawes, thanks for the encouragement and always keeping in touch. Mack Clark, thanks for the support and encouragement. Charlie Pugh, thanks for introducing me to "First Friday" and for being "the voice" for my projects. You're the best!

Linda Burnette, thanks for the sincerity, kindness and positive words of encouragement. Tiffany Pulley, thanks for motivational "boost" and providing resourceful information. Larry Banks, thanks for motivating and inspiring me. Chevez Hawkins, thanks for being so kind, warm and supportive.

Karen R. Johnson, I sincerely appreciate your sincerity and kind words of inspiration. Fritzie Carr, thanks for "checking in" on my progress. I appreciate that. Loretta Nelson, thanks for the love and support. Joseph Perry, your kind words are always priceless. Thanks for your support. Kimberly Boykin thanks for being selfless, inspiring, motivating and loving.

Margaret Boykin and Cordell Scales, thanks for listening to my work and watching my YouTube videos. You're special to me. Alphonso Royals, thanks for your friendship, encouragement and your warm spirit.

Parletta Davis, thank you for always being so supportive and sweet. Thanks for remembering me when it rains. Karen Alexander, thank you for understanding and coaching me during that elevator ride to the 73rd floor! You're priceless. Tanya Hudson, thank you for being fun-loving, supportive and kind. Corliss Fryar, thanks for always being so kind, imparting positive words and supporting my YouTube! Rosalyn Alonzo, I could never forget how you encouraged me, answered all of my questions and helped to calm

my nerves. Thanks, lady! I was real close to skipping town! I appreciate you! Parletta, Karen, Tanya, Corliss, Rosalyn; thanks for being such awesome women!

Marie Norman Harris, thank you for the friendship, laughter, warmth and kind words.

Corneal Tarver, thanks for the encouragement and for listening to everything I've written. Thanks for being my biggest fan and always inquiring about what is next. Reginald Love, thank you for friendship and motivating me to be the best I can be.

Cassandra Kelly, thanks for the 2-, 3-and sometimes 4-hour conversations over the phone: laughing, talking, and enjoying life. You're my girl.

Stephanie Fambro, thank you so much for everything. You are a bundle of joy and always "Stephanie". I wouldn't trade your friendship for anything. Julia and Adolphus Beal, you both make me smile!

Teretha Berry, you are still a "fireball." Thank you for always being so kind, loving and supportive. You're family. Thanks for being you.

Adorna Wilson, thank you for being such a wonderful friend and a great support system over the years. I love you, girl!

Derrick Wills of ID Graphics, Inc. thanks for your encouragement, great designs, patience and professionalism throughout this entire process.

Damon Danielson of Divine Image Graphics thanks for having a creative mind and performing great work!

My cousins, Rev. Kenny and First Lady Azzie Gouch, thanks for the laughs, great times and the "free counseling session." I thank God for you!

Last but certainly not least, I want to thank everyone I could not list, including family, friends, co-workers, cousins, church members, and so many more. Each of you have encouraged and inspired me in many ways. I have drawn strength from each of you throughout our crossed paths. From the bottom of my heart, thank you.

It all would have been impossible without you!

About the Author

Kathy M. Walters is a gem to the literary profession. Though she holds a Master of Science degree in Human Resources Management and an undergraduate degree in Sociology/Criminology and has recently become a Career Development Facilitator, her title of passion is that of an author/poet and publisher. Kathy loves to create and perform poetry as a "window to her soul." Her debut CD, entitled "Speak," is a compilation of smooth music and spoken word that goes hand—in—hand with this piece, *From Pain to Praise, an Inspirational Collection*. Coming soon are an inspirational novella, entitled, *My Cup Runneth Over,* and her sophomore CD, entitled *Simply Love*.

www.ingramcontent.com/pod-product-compliance
Lightning Source LLC
Chambersburg PA
CBHW031548040426
42452CB00006B/240